FINDING FAMILY

The Duckling Raised by Loons

Laura Purdie Salas
illustrated by Alexandria Neonakis

Millbrook Press / Minneapolis

For Vicki and Steve Palmquist, the Game Knights,
and my entire KidLit family —L.P.S.

For Lena, perfect little duckling —A.N.

Millbrook Press™
An imprint of Lerner Publishing Group, Inc.
241 First Avenue North
Minneapolis, MN 55401 USA

For reading levels and more information, look up this title at www.lernerbooks.com.

Back matter photo by Linda Grenzer/the Loon Project.

Designed by Emily Harris.
Main body text set in Mikado Regular.
Typeface provided by HVD Fonts.
The illustrations in this book were created digitally.

Library of Congress Cataloging-in-Publication Data

Names: Salas, Laura Purdie, author. | Neonakis, Alexandria, illustrator.
Title: Finding family : the duckling raised by loons / Laura Purdie Salas ; illustrated by Alexandria Neonakis.
Description: Minneapolis, MN, USA : Millbrook Press, an imprint of Lerner Publishing Group, Inc., [2023] |
    Includes bibliographical references. | Audience: Ages 5–10 | Audience: Grades 2–3 | Summary: "Discover
    the true story of an unlikely family—an orphaned mallard duckling raised by a pair of loons. Lyrical verse
    and evocative illustrations combine in this heartwarming tale of animal cooperation" —Provided by
    publisher.
Identifiers: LCCN 2022020290 (print) | LCCN 2022020291 (ebook) | ISBN 9781728442990 (lib. bdg.) |
    ISBN 9781728485546 (eb pdf)
Subjects: LCSH: Loons—Behavior—Juvenile literature. | Loons—Anecdotes—Juvenile literature. |
    Ducklings—Anecdotes—Juvenile literature.
Classification: LCC QL696.G33 S25 2023 (print) | LCC QL696.G33 (ebook) |
    DDC 598.4/42—dc23/eng/20220603

LC record available at https://lccn.loc.gov/2022020290
LC ebook record available at https://lccn.loc.gov/2022020291

Manufactured in the United States of America
1-50127-49811-7/15/2022

Perched on the edge
of a northern lake,
a nest of dried mud and grass
cradles two eggs.
Olive-colored,
black-splotched
future
loons.

Mother and Father loon
        guard the nest
that rests
        in the shadow
of the tamarack.
Bald eagles patrol the sky.
They spy,
shriek,
and swoop.

JUNE 14

On a stormy day,
eggshell fragments
scatter over nest and water.
A shard here,
a scrap there,
but . . .

where are the chicks?

There!

Mother and Father
hover over
one
scruffy
yellowish chick that
bobbles in the downpour.

But . . .

just one?

Where is the second chick?

Snatched

by snapping turtle or northern pike,

lurking below the water's surface?

Nobody knows.

Mother and Father
dote on their young
one.
Summer
is for raising
a family.

The chick grows.

The chick changes.

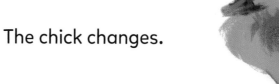

The chick is
  not a loon chick.
  Not from this nest.
  Not from an olive-colored egg.

The chick is . . .

a mallard duckling!

But
where's her mother?
Where's the rest of her brood,
bobbing on the water like tub toys?
And . . . what happened to the two loon chicks?

Nobody knows.

Loons and mallards—
    not close relatives
        nor close neighbors.
            More like enemies.
But gliding through rippling stripes of
      pine,
        maple,
          and aspen,
the unlikely family sails the lake.

Duckling learns loon ways.
Over and over,
Mother and Father
dive down,
rise up
with
        fish.
            Duckling snatches the
        tiny silver slivers.
Mallards don't eat minnows
or take food from their parents . . .
but Duckling does.

She dives,
like Mother and Father.
She surfaces
with a tasty snail!

Mallard bones are not loon-heavy,
pulling them into the deep.
Mallards
rarely
dive . . .
but Duckling does.

Duckling rides piggyback!
She climbs on board Mother or Father and
            poses
like the captain of a ship.
Mallard young don't know their fathers,
and they don't ride piggyback . . .
but Duckling does.

Still, Duckling is a duckling,
  and she does duckling things
    that loon chicks don't.
She dabbles
  in the shallows,
    tipping over,
    dipping half underwater,
    tail waggling like a flag overhead.
She eats weeds and seeds,
  worms and dragonflies.

Duckling dabbles on her own and
eats fish from her parents.
Duckling has all the knowledge she needs
to be part of this family.
        Until . . .

One day, a stranger emerges from fog.
A single loon, searching for a lake of his own.
All young loons know to hide when
a stranger comes.
But Duckling doesn't know.
Father and Mother rush
to confront the trespasser:
      Don't steal our lake!
Duckling doesn't hide.

She splashes toward Father and Mother,
    raising a ruckus,
        putting their home at risk.
Father and Mother scare off the intruder for now,
but will he return
    to fight
        for this territory?

Nobody knows.

Duckling grows large.
Mother and Father

    float low in the water
       under her weight.

           She ventures farther.
           She used to follow her parents
           so-close-a-minnow-couldn't-swim-between.

Now Duckling explores

and nibbles

and cruises along.

And Mother and Father scramble to stay close.

Duckling is practically full-grown.
Soon, parents and young will fly south,

    separately.

As loon families do.
As most mallard families do.

So many questions remain.
What made a pair of loons
    raise a young, lost mallard?
How did a mallard duckling learn loon behaviors?
    Will Duckling find a mallard mate?
    Will Mother and Father loon see Duckling again?

    Nobody knows.

The future is
a perfect mystery
of possibilities,

like an unhatched egg.

Mother and Father and Duckling
  have only now:
a family created
  one dabble and dive,
    one piggyback ride,
      one slippery minnow at a time.

Tonight,
on this clear lake,
under this sunset sky,
with full bellies,
and with family close by . . .
this is enough.

IS THIS STORY TRUE?

In May 2019, a pair of loons nested at the edge of a Wisconsin lake. That lake was part of the Loon Project. Director Walter Piper and his research assistants count, tag, and observe loons each summer in northern Wisconsin and Minnesota. Researchers from the Loon Project carefully record data on the number of loons they see, what sounds they hear, which feeding behaviors they observe, and more.

On a windy, stormy June day, a research assistant who had never seen baby loons before checked on the new family. Afterward, she commented that loon chicks look an awful lot like ducklings. Ten days later, another researcher visited the lake and was astonished to realize that the loons were caring for a duckling, *not* a loon chick!

Piper was also amazed. There was only one other documented case of loons adopting a mallard duckling. "Loons invariably try and drive off mallards . . . they're kind of enemies," he told the National Audubon Society. But these loons were nurturing the duckling instead.

We don't know exactly how the family formed, but Piper speculated that the loons probably lost their chicks to predators. With their parenting hormones at high levels, the adult loons would have been predisposed to care for anything resembling a baby loon. Enter the duckling. There were mallard families on the lake, but nobody knows how this duckling got separated from its own family. We just know the loons and the duckling found each other.

Duckling and her loon parents on July 2, 2019

Researchers observed the family twenty-one times over the summer, and they shared their observations on the Loon Project's website. Readers were charmed by the story and photos, and soon reporters approached the researchers. News stories about the family appeared in magazines and newspapers, and everyone wanted to meet these celebrity waterbirds. The Loon Project released a false lake name to protect the family from news teams and bird-watchers.

On August 19, a researcher observed the family for the last time. Loons and mallards migrate in late summer and early autumn, and by September 4, all three birds were gone. What happened to the duckling? Did it join other mallards that were migrating to the southern United States? Did it join young loons in the Atlantic Ocean? The Loon Project website has the only answer: "As scientists, we commonly use the very powerful words: 'we do not know.'"

Maybe its unknown ending makes this story even *more* worth telling. In life, we don't know what's going to happen tomorrow. All we know, and all we have power over, is right now.

This is a true story of the "right now" of one summer, when two rival species became a single family in the Northwoods wilderness. I relied extensively on research notes and photos from the Loon Project (which correspond to the dates in the story). Those notes, combined with weather databases, expert sources on loon and mallard behaviors, and the kind assistance of Walter Piper and his team, ensured that the story of this surprising family is all fact.

THE INTRUDER

Why was it a big deal when the duckling didn't hide from the intruder loon? Because loons are very territorial, and a good lake is highly valued. The duckling's actions put her family's territory at risk.

In July and August, single loons with no mate search for mates and good breeding lakes. When they spot a pair of loons with a chick, they know the lake is a desirable one, full of delicious fish and invertebrates. A single loon might battle the same-gender loon parent, kick it off the lake, and take over its family. Or it might kill the loon chicks. Or it might just note the lake's location and return to claim the territory the following spring.

It's no surprise that loon parents try to escape the notice of single loons. When one flies overhead, loon parents go to the middle of the lake, where they pretend to be chickless. Meanwhile, loon chicks hide near the shoreline. These actions proclaim, "No chicks here! This lake is not worth stealing!"

But the duckling didn't hide. Instead, says Piper, it "raced towards [the] middle of the lake, while peeping loudly, making itself very obvious." Luckily, the baffled intruder flew away. But even though the intruder would know the duckling wasn't a loon chick, the parents' protective behavior might still have sent a signal: "This lake is great for a loon family. Come back next year to steal it!" Because loon pairs often return to the same lake year after year, losing their lake would jeopardize their own ability to hatch chicks the following year.

VERY DIFFERENT BIRDS

Common loons and mallard ducks are two North American waterbirds that are very different from each other. In fact, the most recent common ancestor of loons and ducks lived about ninety million years ago. Maybe you've never seen a common loon. They spend summers in the wilderness lakes of the far north and winters along North American coastlines. Mallard ducks, however, are truly common across North America. If you see a duck on a lake or a river, there's a good chance it's a mallard.

Loons and mallards also differ in anatomy and behavior. These distinctions make this loon-mallard family truly astonishing.

LOON

closest relatives: penguins and pelicans

population: about 500,000 to 700,000 in North America

red eyes

sharp bill

heavy bones (for diving)

very clumsy on land

carnivorous: eats fish, frogs, leeches, insects, etc.

dives underwater to find food

both parents raise young

parents feed chicks directly

parents give piggyback rides

1–2 chicks in family

chases mallards away

sometimes attacks mallard ducklings

BOTH

waterbird

webbed feet

feathers

wings

bill

nests on land

can swim right after hatching

migrates

MALLARD

closest relatives: geese and swans

population: more than 9 million in North America

brown eyes

rounded bill

hollow, light bones

walks easily on land

omnivorous: eats snails, water plants, grasses, etc.

finds food in shallow water or on land

mother raises young

ducklings find their own food

mother rarely gives piggyback rides

up to 13 chicks in family

SELECTED BIBLIOGRAPHY

Daley, Jason. "Empty-Nester Loons Adopt a Mallard Chick in Northern Wisconsin." *Smithsonian*, July 26, 2019. https://www.smithsonianmag.com/smart-news/empty-nester-loons-adopt-mallard-chick-northern-wisconsin-180972736/.

Mandelbaum, Ryan F. "A Mallard Duckling Is Thriving—and Maybe Diving—Under the Care of Loon Parents." *Audubon*, July 12, 2019. https://www.audubon.org/news/a-mallard-duckling-thriving-and-maybe-diving-under-care-loon-parents.

Piper, Walter. Email correspondence with the author, from December 5, 2019 to May 2, 2022.

"Unlikely Allies," "A Duckling Reared by Loons Enjoys the Best of Both Worlds," "The Amazing Diving Duckling," "The Perils of Interspecific Parenting," and "What Happened to the Duckling." Loon Project. Accessed December 4, 2019. https://loonproject.org/.

FURTHER READING

Bauer, Marion Dane, and John Butler. *A Mama for Owen*. New York: Simon & Schuster Books for Young Readers, 2007. Based on true events, this story is about a tortoise who adopts a baby hippo after a natural disaster.

Buckley, Carol. *Tarra & Bella: The Elephant and Dog Who Became Best Friends*. New York: Puffin, 2014. The true story of a retired circus elephant that makes no friends in the elephant sanctuary—until she meets a stray dog. Includes photos.

The Loon Project https://loonproject.org/ Find factual information about loons as well as updates on loon research carried out in Wisconsin and Minnesota.

Pearson, Yvonne. *Little Loon Finds His Voice*. Oakland, CA: The Collective Book Studio, 2021. In this fictional picture book, a young loon wants to learn to emulate his papa's long, strong calls.

Salas, Laura Purdie, and Chuck Dayton. *Secrets of the Loon*. Saint Paul: Minnesota Historical Society, 2020. A loon chick learns it has all the skills to be independent in this rhyming story based on accurate loon development.

ACKNOWLEDGMENTS

Special thanks to Dr. Walter Piper of Chapman University/the Loon Project, for answering my many questions about this loon-mallard family; to Linda Grenzer, for sharing her loon-mallard images and videos with me during my writing process and for allowing us to share her work in the back matter; and to everyone at the Loon Project for their work with this fascinating species. The Loon Project is primarily funded by the National Loon Center in Crosslake, MN, as well as by private donations. Great thanks also to editor Carol Hinz, who asked if I might be interested in writing a picture book about this unusual family and who championed this manuscript even though it couldn't offer all the answers.